Chandramohan's poetry is an extraordinary combination of a strong individual voice, crying out against a deeply felt sense of personal abuse, and a sophisticated understanding of the long history and mythology of such abuse, in India but also in the world at large. Mythological figures like Shambuka and Urmila illluminate, and are illuminated by, modern atrocities. The poems are by turns shocking, moving, and exhilarating.
— **Wendy Doniger**, *Mircea Eliade Distinguished Service Professor of History of Religions, University of Chicago*

Chandramohan S has the stark ability as a poet to react to any social happening, and these turn out to be in the most responses to societal happenings, plunged into the dark interiors of human behavior. So, these could be related to caste oppression. Economic exploitation, religious polemics etc. But the poetic ability or the agility is always there to handle a situation born out of politico- social situations. There lies his remarkable dexterity as a poet commentator. His lines are direct, and even angry. But that does not matter. This is poetry — at its best. No wonder then that, his poems have been published worldwide. He is perhaps now one of the very few, if not the only Indian poet in English to have taken the burden of social and political repression, as a distinct and livid political idiom. To read his poems is also painful, but the poetry is in the pain!
— **Ananya S Guha**, *Senior Academic in the Indira Gandhi National Open University*

Chandramohan's poems are dialogues of the ' self' with the 'other'. He brings to life a world that subverts myths, literary canons, gender and caste stereotypes by pooling in sparklingly new metaphors with sensitivity and care. He draws his images from contemporary incidents as well as myths and legends of yore, and delves deep into the politicized realm, thus 'rupturing the hymen of demarcations' of identity, resistance, repression and love.
— **Babitha Marina Justin,** academic, writer and artist

LOVE after BABEL

LOVE AFTER BABEL

CHANDRAMOHAN S

Daraja Press

OTTAWA

Published by Daraja Press
https://darajapress.com

© 2020 Chandramohan S
All rights reserved

Cover design: Kate McDonnell
Illustration: Engraving by Jan Luyken, 1705, Rijksmuseum, Amsterdam

Library and Archives Canada Cataloguing in Publication

Title: Love after Babel : and other poems / by Chandramohan S
Names: Chandramohan S. (Chandramohan Sathyanathan), 1986- author.
Identifiers: Canadiana (print) 20190165812 | Canadiana (ebook) 20190165855 | ISBN 9781988832371 (softcover) | ISBN 9781988832388 (ebook)
Classification: LCC PR9499.4.C53 L68 2019 | DDC 821/.92—dc23

Contents

Preface	xi
Acknowledgements	xiii
Introduction: Orienting Dalitality Suraj Yengde	xiv

Part I. CALL ME ISHMAIL TONIGHT

Thirteen ways of looking at a black burkini	3
Thirteen ways of looking at a black beard	5
Before your interrogation	8
When cops come to frisk you	9

Part II. 'NAME ME A WORD'

Killing the shambuka	13
Priest craft	14
Kiss of love	15
Love in the time of CCTV	16
Namdeo Dhasal's letter to a young poet	17
Beef poem	18
The immigrant word	20
Land for the tiller	21
The other	22
Why do I write poetry?	23
License to kill	24
Why loiter?	25
The life and times of Jesus	26

The rape and murder of a tribal	27
Glass ceiling: A new language	28
Portrait of the poet as a young woman	29
Make in India	34
History	35
Kerala Dalit Panther	40
Nangeli	41
The earth	43
A local train conversation (1)	45
A local train conversation (2)	46
Plus-sized poem	47
Draupadi's wedlock(s)	48
Grapes of wrath	49
My psychological lynching	50
Life has to go on	51
Elegy for the slain bloggers	52

Part III. 'LEARNING FROM THE PANTHERS'

Learning from the Panthers	55

Part IV. LOVE after BABEL

(1)	61
(2)	62
(3)	63
(4)	64
(5)	65
(6)	66
(7)	67
(8)	68
(9)	69
(10)	70

(11)	71
(12)	72
(13)	73
(14)	74
(15)	75
(16)	76
(17)	77
(18)	78
(19)	79
(20)	80
(21)	81
(22)	82
Afterword Ananya Wilson-Bhattacharya	83
About the author	90

Preface

I have been writing poetry in the English language for about five years and have achieved reasonably good acclaim and praise from my peers. I continue to explore the world through my own poetry as well as in my role as a translator and curator of contemporary poetry in Malayalam, the other Indian language in which I have roots.

I write from the perspective of a *Dalit* poet writing in English; Dalit is the term of political self-identification for India's independent indigenous peoples and those—previously called "untouchables"—who have historically occupied the lowest rungs of the subcontinent's caste hierarchies. I intend to bring into my poems a wealth of experience from my involvement in various civil right struggles of *Dalit-Bahujans* and also a parallel exploration of intricacies of language in a post-colonial, multi-cultural world. To be frank, Indian writers in English tend to be nearly exclusively from the upper castes. Poets of my background and socio-political leanings tend to be a rarity on the contemporary Indian English poetry scene.

Given that being a Dalit poet comes inextricably intertwined with a subaltern ethos, and given that writing in English language has come to be emblematic of privilege and access to power, I can't but sometimes see myself divided into aspects of privilege and deprivation, colonial and mother tongue. This means my writing inevitably contains elements of self-translation, which in turn offers the audacious possibility for a positive and radical reconstitution of oneself and one's own identity. It is in this context that I have recently been working on a book length poem that explores translation.

Since at least 1972, when the *Dalit Panthers*—a literary as much as political organization—became the last chapter of the Black Panthers, there has been a substantial empathy between Dalit and African American literature; Dalit is a state of existence in India similar to the that of the African-American in the western hemisphere with the added dimension of "spatial pollution". Dalit communities—deemed "untouchable" and "unapproachable"—are still segregated in many parts of India and relegated to the ghettos. I consider myself lucky in that my family has overcome insurmountable odds to bring me to where I am today.

Although autobiography has not yet played a large part in my writing, I have certainly been shaped by the personal experience of being Dalit in my part of India. Even today, I've heard my grandmother being called by her personal name—normally a younger person calling someone much older by their personal name would be considered derogatory in India culture— and many of our non-Dalit neighbors would not consume a drop of water or a morsel of food from our homes even if we are financially slightly more prosperous and better educated with more of our family working in respected government positions. This shows how social exclusion can be immune to mere (relative) economic prosperity. I hope to continue writing poems in English that explore this grim and intense collective experience of social exclusion and humiliation, albeit in formally innovative ways. My poems may well be among the very first to such ordeals of caste in Indian English poetry from the "inside."

Chandramohan S
Trivandrum, May 2020

Acknowledgements

First and foremost, I would like to thank my publisher Firoze Manji of Daraja Press for this unimaginable opportunity to showcase my poems. Without his help this collection would have been impossible.

I thank Mr. K Satchidanandan, Ravishankar N, Babitha Marina Justin, Syam Sudhakar and Vivek Narayanan and many others who have encouraged me with their valuable suggestions and feedback on my poems. I thank Mr. Sudharshan Ketkerry , my first publisher, Jaydeep Sarangi, Subodh Sarkar, Neerav Patel, Kavita Krishnan and Runoko Rashidi whose words and deeds have made this collection possible. I am thankful to Mr. V.Divakar, editor of *The Baroda Pamphlet*, for providing a wonderful platform for my poetry. I also remember Deeptha Achar and Anju Christine, my editors at various points in time. I thank PK Rosi Foundation for the being the oasis of livelihood. I also thank *Poetry Chain* – an initiative by Mr. Gopi Krishnan Kottor for the much-needed feedback, not to forget my closest confidants in poetry, George R and Mathew Jasper. I also thank Ms. Cynthia Stephen, my older sister in Dalit poetry, also comrades Yogesh Maitreya, Aparna Lanjewar, Aruna Gogulamanda. My thanks to Suraj Yengde for the well-thought introduction and Ananya Wilson Battacharya for the afterword, and Ms Wendy Doinger for the blurb that inspires one and all.

I do not intend to forget Soni Somarajan, Meera Nair, Gita Nair, Suneetha Balakrishnan, AJ Thomas, George Szirtes, Philip Nikolayev, Andy Jackson, Bill Herbet. Thank also to KS Bijukumar and Christopher Merril and my other colleagues at the University of Iowa for gifting me confidence in my writing. Comrades Umar, Faisal and Usman: we may get together in India soon.

Chandramohan S
Trivandrum
May 2020

Introduction: Orienting Dalitality

SURAJ YENGDE

Love after Babel is a book not to miss. This brilliant new poetry collection by up-and-coming Dalit poet Chandramohan S shadows through the somber pathways that has large foot marks of the oppressor who has just assaulted our conscience as his quotidian ritual, as if harassing us is his daily chore. As if everyday exploitation is not enough, the oppressor-rapist uses structure to exercise atrocities regularly committed against India's most vulnerable people. The oppressor's boredom is a curse for a peace-espousing humanity.

Love after Babel is propaedeutic—a metaphorical introduction to the vast Dalitness that is concerned with the universal totems and humanist good of all. Dalitness is the radical push of Dalits to validate their agenda in the erstwhile ignored spaces. It is a process of reconciliation with ourselves—compassionate, ignorant and ill-willed. A stitched world of acceptance that has woven together multitudes of identities and their representation in histories. The debonair poet, Chandramohan connects us to the meeting points of the tender touch that marked the beginning of beautiful human fraternity routed through the Dalit expression of the world.

The touch of Genesis 1:26[1] remained in solitary, yet the eleven beholders imagined by the great Michelangelo kept an unflinching eye to the act of touch that might have been witness to the birth of humanity. Yet the yearning, the distance and the dissonance of the new world was made to live in gratis—nothing to be indebted to. The birth of

---

1. KJV: "And God said, Let us make man in our image, after our likeness: and let them have dominion over the fish of the sea, and over the fowl of the air, and over the cattle, and over all the earth, and over every creeping thing that creepeth upon the earth."

western geographies' in the Greco-Roman imagination identified the Others. The masters and slaves—the Greeks and Barbarians were the wholesome selling rapid epithets as philosophies. Aristotle thought of many parts of the world the Africa, Asia, Americas, eastern Europe 'Slavs' as physically ill, mad people fit to be ruled.[2] This was furthered by the rampant colonization of Christianity in the native world whereby stripping of one's individual agency exposed to a higher authority was granted a sacred status. Thus, the lineage of criminalizing people in the bio-politics rendered a tradition wherein an entire clan with certain names were held responsible for criminalizing every other thing that came into their sight. In this logic, Jesus would stand in the court room today appealing for justice at the hands of anti-god heathens. As the poet reminds us Jesus' kids now "sue" the soothsayers as unwanted devils. Caste then stands in the courtyard mocking the principles of justice.

Love after Babel is a highly charged political treatise best told in the language no other art form could have managed to—in poetry. The poet is aware of the dangers of being the Other, but also cognizant that there is no option to be anything but the marked Other. The collection demonstrates how the right-wing ultra-policing culture of surveillance has brought us to a stage where Muslim women's exercising of bodily autonomy in choosing to wear burkinis has been met with widespread racist and Islamophobic backlash. So how, then, does one live the world? Because living the world has coded rules that need to be strictly followed. There are danger zones for the unwanted with growing apartheid policies in distribution and consumption of an open market culture that is Orientalizing the neoliberal order. Living *in* the world, however, is easy. We just need to fit and accept it is our destiny and stfu.

Therefore, there is an oscillation of a tumultuous order. How, then, does one try to be an authentic self when the rabid gaze of the oppressor is hetero-normalizing everything by creating a binary of a double consciousness? Chandramohan suggests that the razor—that we use

---

2. Peter Garnsey, *Ideas of Slavery from Aristotle to Augustine* (New York: Cambridge University Press, 1996)

for trimming the wilderness —has a defined purpose now: to avoid the cops from profiling as there are "thirteen ways of looking at a black beard" (9). The beard is as black as the ground soil. It has a hi(s)tory of the oriental. The erstwhile celebrated identity of manhood and that of warriors, beard is now under the scrutiny if it is pitch-dark color and not Nordic[3]. The immigration official starts counting reasons to humiliate the black beard and suspecting the man's past and his future intentions solely based on the kind of beard he sports. It is a tremendous tension and mind-exercise for one to have the beard. To avoid the national assault better to shave. This has divided the civilization and maps are redrawn, by going against the geographical sanity and historical routes. The poet brutally charges,

> some islands changed hands
> Between their imperial masters
> No river changed course

Non-Western and marginalized identities are a prime target for the new western that proudly harks on its derogatory ancient values professed through racist appetite and caste blood of affected Dalit. Therefore, giving up one's caste identity—the history of one's belonging is the only way forward for the helpless who seeks to camouflage for self-protection—much to its displeasure. Chandramohan brings back the discussion of the black body that is further inferiorized for its naturality. He uses dreadlocks as a metaphor for the physical display of marginalised identity— the damning biometric euthanasia that can even trace your "footprint from the sands" (6). Had it been for privacy only, the banks, corporations, feudals, casteists, racists, homophobic, transphobic, sexist everyone would have created a movement to abolish it. Data is the new Orwellian world where mind of individual is in the hands of corporate-serving-states.

But the poet, Chandramohan is optimistic. What else does he have to offer if not optimism and futuristic promises? He simply cannot dwell on the manipulated past. Thus, he is hopeful that after his and our

---

3. Trump desired immigrants from Norway as opposed to the immigrants from 'shithole countries'.

collective death history will bear the witness on the scale of justice trying to catch up with us. What can the future, unborn generation do? They will memorialize us and erect monuments in our honor. History still will remain second-rate produce of the seer. History is an alter-ego for the poet that is high on ganja; sharp in thought, lost in precision. The reasons are apparent as he holds the mirror:

> Does a wound/childhood scar
> Have a dispute ancestry?

After every tragedy, finding the Other's global caste becomes the business of the ruffians who are bought in to system of oppression making a self-belief of superiority As the poet reminds us,

> Before the twin towers fell
> Some surnames were innocuous.
> After the fall
> Some surnames are fish-bones.

Through variant panoramic openings, Chandramohan has offered us a critique of global casteism operating under the name of xenophobia where answers with mono-syllables are preferred. We—the rest of the wretched 'us' – cannot own a narrative. Our democracy is to celebrate the orgasm of kings & queens of our worlds—the traditional elite aristocrats and welcome their new specimen hoping that they will grow into benign leaders to govern our grandchildren's societies.

Life is decrying the persistence of the past—the bygone tombstone of erstwhile rulers. Looking back with full-bodied movement is a taxing work and so the best one can do is lend the gaze by blinking the eyes upwards in the rear-view mirror. And who's catching up? It is the unforgiving history. Beware: it knows all. You cannot claim ignorance, for it will discipline you too. Rear-view sits at the center of centipede Fordist Machiavellianism dotted with alarming signs of age-old stigma still attached to the newer inventions. That once heckled body now continues to be stigmatized in a million-dollar car. Rear-view mirror is useless. It is just a reminder of the inescapability of a deeply disturbing past. For Chandramohan it figures in description of revolutionary treatise of burkini, the colonized' black beard, and in the age of anti-blackness the state following like a sore-loser trying to catch up the growth of black genius.

Blood of caste-hymens

This collection of ideas weaved into fragments of words is a serious philosophical treatise. It is a bountiful addition to the glowing rebellious poetic scenery. We need it for the nourishment of our malnourished souls. The poems are a line passing through like a piercing sunlight trying to escape the dungeons of a dusty room that is clouded with the sweat and ugliness of ideas whose life-world no one knows. They're archives for the curious one—the history-less toiler; for the rest—the freeloaders of toiler's labor —they are simply dust-laden asthma prone papers who're bringing uncontrollable sneezes of one's disapproval. The dust is organized debris of Chandramohan's madness to love in a hateful society

There are dancing metaphors woven into a language the poet is sensitive about. The glass window of a deserted mansion is described the "tetanus to your soul" (88). Transparent and dusty, yet proclaiming special superiority in the times of inflated? Housing market prices. The seeming contradiction with the vernacular vs. colonial grants a pass for the earlier to reclaim self. But to do what? To reestablish cultural hierarchy in a divided world where global Brahmins are desperate to bring their oppressive order. Chandramohan teases us with a description of the now-moment that is gathering of a foregone era where "history of mankind is snor[ing] in my language (89)."

In his radical best, the poet dares us to think about the 'Priest Craft' carried out by the dominating Brahmins. These vanguards of the "Caste hymens" are afraid of the Dalit sperms that can shower upon the fire of casteism. Because a love-making act, as the poet argues, has the power to change the course of time. The time that has ensured its own supremacy over contemporary experiences.

Erecting romantic rebellion

Chandramohan has managed to convey deep historical meaning to our current conditions. His references are admiringly wild and sweeping. They are important and urgent. One needs to pay heed to his warning – otherwise "...half decomposed corpse[s] (will) resurface on a pond" (44). The reality will be revealed. Beware! you. Yes, it is you who is continues to play the role of liberal or radical yet remain casteist to the core. What good is your ideology if it is not destroying the caste system.

Chandramohan's poetry comes to life packed with posies revealing many hidden meanings. It is stoic, rebellious, confrontational, revolutionary, feminist, humanistic, romantic, intimate. At the core of it happily sits Dalitality—an essence of embracing the vulnerability of others.

The poetry is an abstraction that we so desperately need to address the problems at hand. The poems refuse to be castigated into someone else's imagination. They want to develop their own ontological locus. Thereby, they become a suggestive prophetism written in a revolutionary tradition of Dalitism that shines with the universalism of all.

Chandramohan wears a few more hats in addition to the poet. He is a translator of moments. In this attempt, the poet and translator becomes a philosopher blossoming in the garden of frank park. He subverts the language and tells the hegemon that they're incapable of putting those 26 alphabets into an order to civilize – read colonize – the non-alphabetic dialects. The limited phonetics do not yet capture and are not equipped to dwell on the inner experiences of colonized people. The jargons are far limiting. This language has been systematically enforced even as their own languages and cultures have been, and continue to be snatched away from them. .

The Dalit Panthers of India wrote, and imagined in vernacular. Their vernacularism was rooted in the ground-up problems. The Panthers are a "disciplined men" who are upset – which causes them to "upset the natural order of things". The Panthers' fight is a non-violent attack on oppression, but if they receive strong violence in rebuttal, in response they can militate like the "master of the martial artist" Ambedkar who inspired all of the Dalit humanity and whose skillful punches are directed in self-defense; but also they are outward action to "educate organize and agitate". Ambedkar has discussed the martial history of Dalit castes.[4]

The Panthers' sky-blue flag oozes the aroma of "universal brotherhood"—the maitri, fraternity that the sharp stylist Ambedkar, so earnestly fought for.

One needs to be an admirer of art to fully grasp the depth of the provocations that Chandramohan throws on the canvas of humans' fate. One has to find real reasons in the apparentness of philosophical famine. Only Chandramohan could "script a camaraderie in a cloudless sky". Many will still desire for more such friendships, a supposed antidote to caste-difference. His poems are poetic. They evoke the desire to stare at a silhouette gasping in a heated dust of scorching, fazing day.

The white-only is a stale world for this new poet, who nevertheless looks at colors through *the invasive colonial conceptions* of color lines that produced dualism of white and non-white at the helm of creating a bastardly white-only supremacy for a white-only world. The exploits of the past have legs with which they walk straight into your lives announced. How much can then one go about hiding or creating new myths to hide this domination. Themes of femininity, combined with feminist critique, run throughout the verses like a blood stream. The earth is posed as the mother, the female who is being draped naked

---

4. B R Ambedkar, 'The Untouchables and the Pax Britannica", *Dr. Ambedkar Writings and Speeches*, Vol. 12 (Bombay: Government of Mahrashtra), pp. 75-154. Ambedkar argues that had it not been for the Dalits, English forces would have never seen the sunlight *(a reference to 'the sun never sets in the empire')* that they so proudly claimed *from* the wars against Napoleon, the India conquest from 1757 (Battle of Plassey) to 1818 (Battle of Koregaon), till the squashing of Mutinies of 1857. Untouchables—the Dusads, Mahars, Chamars—fought alongside the invaders, "in the hope that the new comer will release them from the oppressions of their countrymen."

by the serial-caste abusers harming her honor—the mountains, gorges. The whoring of someone's freedom is permanently marked on the 'lower bodies' in the patriarchal hierarchy of the sexes—females.

Evidently, the language is rich, fresh and musical to a funky mind. It is a deep introspective exercise that breaks the boundaries like a rebellious Dalit woman would break the tissues and spines of those who dare to harass her and her family.

A bold call is made for political rights alongside economic. As taxation is on the tongues of every neoliberal political move. The sloganeering of "No taxation without representation" adds up to the "No reparation without representation" shattering the applicants of caste-ist democracy (46). Castes are tied to the blood groups where they won't work if the group is different. What use is a AB+ve to B-ve? Castes are sanctified blood rituals demanding blood of 'lower castes' through guilty means of exploitation.

The contemporary world, struck by a pervasive pessimism, offers respite through the art form of technology, allowing individuals to get lost in the cobwebs of web-ism insinuated by the hardy technology that guarantees freedom of a censored nature. "This page cannot be displayed". "You don't have permission to access." Or simply "Access denied." Everything here is patrolled and policed. Therefore, let's go slow on celebrating the censored democracy of I.T. run by the Government of Google dictated by the enigma of algorithmic untraceable, cunning hands. For Google is again an imperial order where "it could take a long time for you to know who you are, Amidst the web traffic along world's sea routes" before it proclaims itself as an undefeated god of our generation.

The poet has brought out a treatise that acts like a placard on a highway displaying the message: "take care of yourself". What more would one need beyond self-care. However, in an odorous climate of predatory instincts of profiteering that is premised on exploitation of anything and everything that captures your cornea—living or non-living, we need poets like Chandramohan to guide us and warn us, even scold us at times. We also need reminders about the mayhem we're so dearly arrested to.

When we are witnessing unforgiving catastrophes and experiencing bleak everyday realities in the name of climate damage, xenophobia, racism, caste-ism, sexism, homophobia, and transphobia, *undermining* everything that humane values teach us, we need to find moments within poetic art that offer us courage and confidence. We come out of this soul-book more energized and more courageous to commit ourselves to the fight.

Suraj Yengde
Harvard University,
Cambridge, Massachusetts
September 2, 2019

PART I
CALL ME ISHMAIL TONIGHT

Being Arab

*Not for your sake, but
mine, at airports and on planes
I act extra nice.*

By
HayanCharara

Thirteen ways of looking at a black burkini

"I created the burkini to give women freedom, not to take it away "
—Aheda Zanetti

1
Burkini is a language
Terrifying those ignorant of its text.

2
Cops patrol her tan lines
Like dams patrol
Rivers flowing above danger marks.

3
All you need is in that bag:
Change into a garment
More palatable for the cops in uniform.

4
Some garments cling too close to your surname
Like a metaphor
Too loud for good poetry.

5
Sea surfing can be tiring
Like an infinite ebb and flow of a questionnaire.
Batting an eye lid can be a tad too immodest.

6
Tether yourself close to the beach.
Do not surf too deep into the ocean.
Never self-intersect in circles of knots and tangles.

7
Bruises sustained from frisking
Metamorphose into festering wounds.
Gangrene could gnaw at your surname.

8
Erase your footprints from the sands.
Waves of time rarely wash the footprints of a scuffle.
Prolonged scuffle can bury us all in a deep hole.

9
Do you remember the first corpse
The sea sucked off a turbulent beach?
The sea spat it out after three days of frisking.

10
The footprints of scuffle
Implicates you from shore to shore,
Blowing up all bridges between you and anyone.

11
During this conversation
Some territory has been ceded across
The tan lines of your body.

12
Your body stripped off the garment
Remains an evacuated language.
Can a language be a scarecrow?

13
History will catch up with you
In your rear-view mirror
Even if you are full throttle in your
Pursuit of happiness.

Thirteen ways of looking at a black beard

1
Does the razor, shaving
hundreds of beards
cops pull out of line
to frisk, shave its master?

2
All you need is in that bag:
Trim your surname,
Make it palatable for tongues
At the immigration office.

3
Tiny specks of blood
Surf on soap bubbles,
Cuts appear daily
On nameless faces.

4
The blade is twin-edged:
One side for shaving,
The other to redraw maps
Across the world.

5
Cuts on the map of the world
Sewn together is your face
In the mirror.

6
In the midst of this conversation
Some islands changed hands

Between their imperial masters
No river changed course.

7.
Always tether your goat.
Do not fly kites.
Never self-intersect yourself
In knots and tangles.

8
Frisking is not intrusive
But very intimate like
Claws gloved with caresses
Patrol the nerve endings of my civilization.

9
Before being frisked
Pull out from your pockets
Venom of the veins of history
Entombed as sound bite: BOOM!

10
Try loose shunting your name
If it has flammable content:
Don't let the millipede of evolution
Come to screeching halt.

11
Some surnames were innocuous
Before the fall of the twin towers,
After the fall the
Some surnames are fish-bones
Stuck at the throat, never binned:
They hide shameful secrets.
A mustache could grow lop-sided.

12
Your name will be put on trial,
Based on evidence
Obtained from torturing

Unless history intercepts us
Like a bullet split into two
Blinding both our eyes.

13
History will catch up with you
in your rear-view mirror
Even if you are full throttle in your
Pursuit of happiness.

Before your interrogation

When cops come to frisk you,
Drape your soul in mono-syllable answers.

Your forehead doesn't seem to have furrows
Ploughed by your faith?

Please identify all the branches of this family tree
Knotted with your blood.

Start a contraption by curling your hair
Set in motion a perfect identity theft (not robbery)

Wear your patriotism
On your sleeves
Like superman's underwear.

The curves of your body are not analytically tractable
We usurp your roots!

We have to take you to a black hole
Devoid of any reason.

You need to confess
From the Big Bang to the drifting of Pangaea.

Perch on a verse
From a new language
Push the envelope of your horizon.

When cops come to frisk you

1. Batting an eye lid
In the midst of an excruciating questionnaire
Could be a tad too immodest.

2. He could try mock intimidating techniques
Like the cacophony of revving a car
Engine with gear set to neutral.

3. Learn to steady your breath
Like an undercover cop
In a trigger-happy gang.

4. You both have each other's face
To ascertain the time epochs
Each of you is living in—untranslatable in time.

5. He could lop some withered branch
Of your family tree and ask you to
identify the leaves.

6. If he greets you in your rustic dialect,
Return the serve.

7. He may try to ascertain the blood pressure
Of your privilege coursing your veins.

This whole conversation is jarring like a poem translated
Into a language with no word for the missing rib.

PART II
'NAME ME A WORD'

Killing the shambuka

(*Inspired by a famous poem on black lynching*)[1]

Jim Crow segregated hostel rooms
Ceiling fans bear a strange fruit,
Blood on books and blood on papers,
A black body swinging in mute silence,
Strange fruit hanging from tridents.

---

1. This poem draws its inspiration from the poem *Strange Fruit* (1937) by Abel Meeropol and is on the suicides of Dalit-Bahujan students in institutions of higher education in India. RohithVemula is one of the recent victims (Jan 17,2016)

Priest craft

Just like the saying goes—
Tongue has no bones
But can break many,

The submissive tuft of hair on the shaved
Heads of the twice born
Command an army of henchmen
Guarding the rust of
Medieval fences built along
Caste hymens.

Kiss of love

Correct our watches by the public clocks.
Then sit for half an hour and drink our bocks.
—**TS Eliot,** *Portrait of a Lady*

Two pairs of lips
Lock in a kiss
Losing all sense of time.

Heads turn
To adjust wrist watches
From a public clock.

Locked lips
Turn the wheel of time
Like prophets.

Love in the time of CCTV

In my rear view mirror is the motherfucking law.
—**Jay Z**, *99 problems*

(1)[1]
The camera tells us.
Keep your hands where I can see them.
Write your love letter.

(ii)
Of lovers whose bodies smell of each other—T.S.Eliot

Queer pride march
With cops escorting us on either sides
Like every alphabet of the poem
Is being odour-tested
For the scent of the other.

---

1. The title owes its origin to a submission call by a literary platform edited by Sumana Roy and GunjanaDey.

Namdeo Dhasal's letter to a young poet

In your poems
Do not set your rhyme and meter
To the drum beats of populism.

You may build mansions in their shade
Where synthetic grass is cut to level
And flowers bloom in time for the next election season
With petals the teal of the incumbent flags.

Before your mansions crumble,
I want to send you
To the smithy of the blacksmith.

[Postscript: Do not charge fees to read poems on hunger.]

Beef poem

(1)
My harvest of poems
Will be winnowed,
If done deftly
The lighter, shallow poems
Are blown away,
While the meatier, heavier poems
Fall back into the tray,
To become the fire
In my belly like
Beef.

(2)
Mastheads with nausea
Against beef eating
Consider my poems
"untouchable"

(3)
Mastheads
First have vegetarians and non-vegetarians
And then non-vegetarians and beef eaters
On either sides of their lines of horizon.

(4)
For some poets
Beef is the
Locus of all the
Food for thought in the world
Like Buddha's begging bowl.

(5)
When I manoeuvre sharp curves of history
In my rear-view mirror
I see some trucks overfull with cattle
Waiting at the check points
Like strands of fables
Edited out of history textbooks.

(6)
Pressure cooker's whistle
Like one-eyed search light:
Hawk's eye on our bellies.
(7)
A dead cow preserved in formalin
Like Hitler's penis in a museum.
(8)
Beef poems adorn various
Poetic forms like sausages—
Cyanide capsules worn around our necks
(9)
Performances to packed audiences
And end the poem
With a knockout punch
Onto their rib-cages.
(10)
Beef nourishes us
through the recipe of a commune.
(11)
Every time the rage attenuates
I beef up
My poetry.
(12)
My poems are not inert objects
They are verbs of insurrection.
(13)
Beef poems
Like meatballs of beef
With a label of "handle with care"
Like biting the trigger
Of a grenade.
(14)
Discard a myth
Like piece of meat
A vestigial organ being operated upon.

The immigrant word

The immigrant experience for
A word in a poem
Is like being subjected to numerous enunciations
At poetry slams
To rhyme with rest of the poem.

The immigrant experience for
A word in a poem
Is to sound like "Prufrock",
To be conspicuous
Like fly in the buttermilk.

The immigrant experience for
A word in a poem
Is to be accompanied with a footnote
Like the entire poem has a GPS tag
On one of its ankles.

The immigrant experience for
A word in a poem
Is to be a paper boat on the
High tide of strife—
Washed ashore like the corpse of a toddler.

The immigrant experience for
A word in a poem
Is solitary confinement
In the prison of syntax.

The immigrant experience for
A word in a poem
Is an undecipherable tombstone
in the war memorial.

Land for the tiller

A comrade with a red flag
visited our god forsaken colony;
my grandfather parroted his slogan
"land for the tiller".

The old man
tilled the land,
poured out the sweat from his body,
erected the flag firmly on the ground.
The flag was hoisted sky high.
He watched it with moist eyes from 64 feet away.

His deferred dreams
have sprung up today in makeshift tents,
in lease-expired lands of Harrison Malayalam
at Chengara ,Muthanga and Arippa.

The other

In the palette of his hieroglyphic expressions
I decipher a codebook of prejudice.
In the archive of exposed crimson veins in his cornea
I retrieve a manuscript of contempt.
In the superlative adjectives of his flattery
I discover a verb of deception.
In his effervescent smiles
I sense a tinge of alienation.
In his adoring synonyms of deification
I deduce the snobbery of denigration.

Why do I write poetry?

They ask me why do you write poems ?
I write poems -the people have the right to keep and bear arms.
They ask me what new artillery I had invented?
Heckler poems -dynamites at election rallies.

License to kill

Not a morsel of food down her throat
An act of protest against licenses to kill
Her periodic crimson stopped
To stop the crimson rivers flowing down the streets
Of her seven sisters.

Why loiter?

(In the neoliberal world)

The era of open markets
Added colour to the stale world of white-only lingerie,
Everything got spun around
Like the inside of the washing machine,
With the colour pink spilling over to the white,
To scrounge for a rump-sized perch
On the lingerie clothesline.

The life and times of Jesus

(From the Lost Gospel)

The first woman in his life
Was Mary,
His mother.

She was a feminist,
Made love,
Wrote a lullaby for bastard children,
Chanted at protest rallies against
Child abuse by clergymen.

He had married Marie Magdalena
She earned more than her preacher husband,
Wrote a sermon on equal wages for women—
Tried to organize prostitutes.

He had kids.
They sued Friedrich Engels
Disputing the origin of family,
Private property and
The state of the Catholic Church.

The rape and murder of a tribal

No newspaper carried a headline or a photo feature,
No youth were roused to protests,
No city's life came to a standstill,
No furore in the parliament,
No nation's conscience was haunted,
No Prime minister addressed the nation,
No TV channel discussions,
No police officials were transferred or suspended,
No candle light marches,
No billion women rising,
A tribal girl was raped and murdered!

Glass ceiling: A new language

"Although we weren't able to shatter that highest, hardest glass ceiling this time, thanks to you, it's got about 18 million cracks in it." —**Hillary Clinton**

The midnight sky is a dark glass ceiling.
The lightning cracks
Illuminate a new calligraphy.

The deep sea lungs of a cyclone
exhale loud thunderclaps,
a nascent utterance.

Portrait of the poet as a young woman

(for Aruna Gogulamanda)

One is not born, but rather becomes, a woman.
—**Simone de Beauvoir**

1)
Her hair
Freshly harvested dreadlocks
Unedited gospel of love
Off limits to combs.

Tresses like streams
Of eternal fire
From the arsenal of her body.

Her verses braid
Themselves into a halo,
She wears it lightly
With the modesty of a headscarf.

2)
Each of her verse
Has a gridlock of events entwined on it.
She uses them like a skipping rope
To maintain her frame.

Her knotted hair
Un-knots seven colours of light.

Columns of lights
Like rainbow—ribbons
Braided along with her hair
Like unravelling a newly illuminated strand of history.

3)

Her swag
Spills on to her hair
They sway like branches of a tree,
Birds of sunset come to roost.

The parting of her hair into two halves
along the meridians
the illuminate and the unlit
merge into raven black.

She stealthily uncoils herself
Like un-knotting her hair.
Her name is freed from parenthesis.
From now on, her poem
Diffuses into well-knit free-verse.

Her book of poems
A treatise on roots usurped &
Untamed bloodlines.

4)
Her landscape
When unveiled, stretches into various time zones
Like stanzas of her poem.

The stretch marks on her landscape are
The neat furrows on un-tilled land.

Reading her poem
Uninterrupted is like
Innumerable intermittent rivulets
Joining hands to form a perennial river.

The unfurling flutter of her verses
Create low- pressure points
In the waves of time
Foaming into a tornado.

5)
Her breasts are lop-sided
Like the tilted axis of the earth.

Her nipples, twin needles
Perched at eye level
With precision of feline vision.

The nipples with halos
of aureole- ripples emanating
From the core of the earth.

6)
Her face is a mask
Tightly knit to never let out a sigh.
Sensitive to the jagged axes of light
Chiseling her melanin.

7)
If midnight sky is a dark glass-ceiling
Her verses are the
The lightning cracks:
Illuminate a new calligraphy.

Her form of poetry
Is like an unpredictable sequence of thunderclaps
From the deep sea lungs of a cyclone:—
A nascent utterance.

Accents thick like her lips
Sipping curdled mulatto.

8)
Poems conceived in a celestial tongue
When stars align with caesarean precision.
It is our own language.

Her verses
Are neither left nor right aligned
Time zones hinge at every line break
Like sunflowers UNaligned to the scorching heat.

Her swag spills on to her versus
A rivulet of sweat coursing
The sonorous hum of her swaying torso.

Every evening, on her terrace,
She lets her hair down and flies kite,
Her verses tell vivid stories
Stitched together in myriad colours.

Her verses gurgle like rivers let loose.
She never braids them
With her bare hands
Before a poetry reading.

9)
When her poems are read
No boyfriend or pimp is allowed
Inside the reading hall.

But you have an option of signing a peace treaty
With the totem of her tattoo
She flaunts on the sleeves
Of her sleeve-less attire.

Her belly-button is a whirlpool in the river of her language.
It can capsize her readers, venturing deep into her,
Unmindful for her folded undercurrents.

10)
A flower opens her petals
After dusk, folds before dawn
Like a bird always ahead of the sun.

A bird drenched in scarlet
Flies out of her orifice
A wing-clipped lyric.

11)
She foot-taps on the floor
While reading—her feet like
Tyre of an SUV treading a rough terrain.

Bandaged toes—like those of an athlete,
Broken nails with nail polish
Like indicator lights used to manoeuvre sharp curves.

I look at her feet
Like a thirsty man at water—the womb of life,
Or as if in trance over the feat of a primeval woman.

Her kite, un tethered to her surname,
Soars high, till it gets entangled with the stars.

Attempting to translate her poems
Is like making love to a capricious mistress.

12)
While reading her poems
Her pelvis gyrate
Along newer ellipses of epics.

Her wide hips
Birth "*brand new myths*"
With undying ripples as wide as the equator.

Her hissing curly stream of verses
Sway to the rhythm of her gait
Untamed by the clanging of her anklets.

Her book of poems,
A treatise on dishevelled hair
And tresses on fire.

Make in India

(Labour under attack)

The lumpen proletariat.
The sweat of his brow evaporates
To condense in the bottles
Of the beverage corporation.

The frail frame of his wife
Is his daily punching bag.
Does he have a title to defend?

History

1.
In my rear-view mirror
History is on my tail.

Wait.
It isn't even history.
It's my own alter ego following me.

Objects in a convex mirror are
Closer than they seem.
While navigating sharp curves.

Some planets travel slower
Than their average speeds
Near their apogees.

It's called retrograde motion;
Do not sign contracts—
Our intellect takes a well-deserved break.

Ganja in my brain!

2.
We ride a wave
Talk in double-entendre.

Can I use the same convex
Mirror to focus all my rage
On the religious mark on your forehead?

Is the *surplus value* of
The sweat dripping down your
Brow for ages
The secret of your glowing skin?

Insert a "Gospel of the slave tribe"
Post-scripted mythology.

Scarecrows suffuse the
Apartments of the neo-rich.

Can I mount an insurrection
By cascading myths
In my verses?

Build a missile defence shield
Along points of inflexion
To intercept patronization.

Can a series of cascading myths
Surmount an insurrection
Against his self-anointed lineage
Longer than the longest freshwater
Currents of the world?

3.
Does a wound/ childhood scar
Have a disputed ancestry?

Insert a NOTE to the slave tribe
In the tri-junction of mythology
A prosthetic limp for a long
Stroll in the desert.

Should I speak with the proper
Semiotics, as if signing on a bond paper?

An old hidden dialect resurfaces
Like a half-decomposed corpse
Resurfacing on a pond.

4
A clash between "bourgeois sobriety"
And "proletarian frivolities"
At the orthogonal delta of language!

I stammer when I respond to
His abrasive questions.
Horizons hinge on my replies.

A minister used to connive
Amidst his stammer.

Cosmopolitan attire plus sophisticated accent
Tongue rinsed clean of any
Vernacular tinge.

Reptilian circumference of scorpion's sting
An arm's distance at school prayer halls.

Is sight an extension of touch? (A reverted glance!)
Is shadow synchronous with the hourglass?

Does shadow travel faster than light?
Can the nodes of a shadow mar your nuptial bed?

5.
Dark circular patches below your eyes,
Chinks in your aristocratic halo!

Shoulders stoop with the
Senile burden of many epochs.
Can I relieve his shoulders
From the yoke of assumed names?

My strides are like
A swimmer's miniscule scrawls
Against the current.

6.
Educate Agitate Organize!
I have been trained to punch
Above my weight.
Can I strip him off his caste surname?

His name has a tail
Violating the sanctity of my airspace
I chase him down like a fighter pilot.

No gum shield or headgear

It is a long tedious harangue
With insidious intent.

Does my enemy have enemies
Disguised as friends?
Will any of them abstain
From voting during the floor test.

Can I shift from
Active to positive voice
In the midst of a conversation and
Drift to my mother's surname?
A bloodline refugee!

Castes are like egg-yolk.
Scramble them,
They hatch into sub-castes!

Not even a squirm is gravity free.
No taxation without representation.
No reparation without representation.

A belief system collapses
Like a torpedoed ship
Anchored to an intangible myth.

Some blood groups take
Longer to coagulate
The lower one is on the scale
Of contempt.

If the cobbler and toddy tapper
Outshine the blazing sun

Then stake claim on his seed,
The twice-born conspiracy.

Languages are plastic handles
To manoeuvre molten identities
From hot furnaces.

Clean the dirt from the veins of history
Using toilet cleaning poisons.

What if I am half-caste?
Do sperm deposits in sperm banks
Suffer progressive infertility?
A half-moon is still a moon.
The one-drop rule in reverse!

Kerala Dalit Panther

(for K AMBUJAKSHAN)

The panther brothers are coming,
Step aside—let their reign begin.

The panther brothers
Marching shoulder to shoulder
Like alphabets of the same vernacular
Bound together with no vices.

The panther brothers are coming
Like a sun sliding off the eclipse
New rays on the dark recesses of history—
A moustache sprouting on barren land.

The panther brothers are coming;
They are one people:
One language, one history, one culture.

The raised fist
Like the arms of a clock at noon
Turn the wheel of time,
Hoisting the blue flag.

The panther brothers are coming,
Stomping their feet
Like an earthquake from beneath
The voice of the silenced roots.

The panther brothers are coming,
The veins under their black skin
Long like the river Nile,
Ancient like the river Indus.
The same veins as the curly-haired Buddha.

Nangeli

Twin voluble streams of blood
Flow from the festering wounds of Nangeli[1]
With the semi-divine fury of Kannagi.

The tax-collector wailed
And howled like a wild animal
For the streams to stop.

The streams flowed unabated.
Meanwhile, her husband had drowned
In one of the streams.

The district collector ordered
The streams to be handcuffed
And tied to a giant banyan tree.

The streams refused to budge.

The priest of the local temple
Decreed the streams to go dry—
Conjured them to bleed to death.

The streams did not coagulate.

A tent was erected.
Organising committees formed.
The Akalis opened canteens.
The messiah of non-violence arrived.
Still the deity was off limits to sunlight.

---

1. The village-legend of Nangeli is about an "intermediate caste" woman who lived in the early 19th century at Cherthala (Alapuzha District, Kerala) in the princely state of Travancore in India. She supposedly, cut off her breasts in an effort to protest against a caste-based "breast tax". Her grandchildren survive to this day. Source:https://www.thehindu.com/news/cities/Kochi/200-years-on-nangelis-sacrifice-only-a-fading-memory/article5255026.ece

The streams did not fold in supplication.

The streams flow to this day.
The cartographers always miss it.

The twin streams are
Couplets of a people's poet
Transcending her untimely death
At the high tide of her rhythm.

Nangeli is the engraver, and the
Moon is menstruating.

The earth

Adorns herself alternately
In her thick foliage of green and
The capricious ebb and flow of blue.

Each geologist weaves a
Garment for her curves of
Mountains and gorges,
Like a layer of dense air.

I start unwrapping her layers of drapery.
They are plaits of soiled bedsheets
Branching out from her midriff like
Tributaries of a river
Near its delta.

She hides herself
In different layers of meaning
Through its mantles
Like an epic revolving around
A rainbow-like narrative axis.

Scrolls of scriptural injunctions
Ooze from her orifices with the hiss of uncoiling snakes.

Certain inner layers are like
Holy books,
Light once trapped
Never escapes: illuminated for eternity!

I discover cavities
As wide as the
Hips of Venus
Or the chest of mars.

The heat from the earth's core

Drives the machinery of
My muse.

A local train conversation (1)

(Version one)

As the station moves
I glance at the
Elderly man seated opposite me
Still like an inanimate cog in a wheel.

His religious mark between his eye-brows
A one-eyed search light
Patrolling for moon-light indiscretions
Down the ages as the train furrow
Through a dimly lit tunnel.

His insidious queries
Incised with his Swiss-knife tongue
Are like a handshake
Prolonged to probe
The pulse of my wrist.

He tries assessing me with an in swinger first
"What is your full name?"

Then he tries an out swinger that seams a lot
"and what is your father's name?"

By this time, he loses his nerve
And tries on a swift yorker
"What is your caste?"

A local train conversation (2)

(Version Two)

Caste in a local train can be deceptive
Like the soul of a Pakistani fast bowler
Camouflaged in a three piece suit
And anglicized accent.

Though seated opposite me
I can feel him charging on to me.

I try to decipher the totem
Inscribed in his religious marks amidst his eyebrows
Like trying to find my way around
An ever changing map!

He sets the ball rolling with some seemingly
Innocuous remarks-like a warm up exercise
Before a duel of queries and answers
Or like the casting of a die.

He scratches on the line of his horizon
Using the sting at the end of his twilit queries.

He tries extrapolating the curvature of my answers
To curve-fit a new orbit for our shared world.

He tries assessing me with an in swinger first
"What is your full name?"

Then he tries an out swinger that seams a lot
"What is your father's name?"

By this time he loses his nerve
And tries on a swift yorker
"What is your caste?"!

Plus-sized poem

This poem refuses to be
The world's wife.

This poem is not pimple-free,
Is printed on rough paper.

This poem has cellulite in its rear end,
Its rump outsizes itself off the market.

This poem walks the ramp with a self-edited gait
Without introduction or foreword from veterans.

This poem does not opt for offshore liposuction
To make oneself eligible for international prizes.

This poem eludes the trap
In the hourglass of time.

Draupadi's wedlock(s)

for ApekshaGhatkar

Tethered to a wedlock of five keys
Each made of a different element

A padlocked shared fortress
Forced-upon every time the sun sets.

Bruises near the key-hole-
Inscriptions of a drunken stupor.

A pair of lips dodging a kiss
Like a couplet eluding translation.

Her name splits into five-fold heteronym
Encircling her like petals of a flower.

The wedding ring like a key-hole—
A peep reveals a deep gorge- like a ringed well.

The wedding- garland thick
Like forearms of five men on her shoulders

The weakest link of an unbroken chain of command
From mother-in-law to the bride-to-be.

Grapes of wrath

(A poem on migrant labourers in Kerala)

> *The displaced of capital have come to the capital.*
> —**Anne Winters**

Faceless migrant lads
Tread landscapes of tongues
To be greeted with a lisping embrace
At God's own country.

My psychological lynching

I was watching a movie the other day,
the hero hailing from the slums
speaks in 'uncouth' slang,
his Anglo Saxon girlfriend sets in right
with a tight slap!

From then on
The hero sways in sync with his heroine,
a paler version of his former self.
Keep the body, take the mind.
The psychological lynching of my soul.

Life has to go on

(For the Paris Terror Attack)

Who are the suicide bombers sneaking into a poem?

Maybe it was the vernacular river
Buried deep under a sign board
That had seceded from the poem
To become a landmine.

Maybe it is the tongue
Spoken by the vanquished minority
Bent like a question mark
To touch the feet of the despot
Before triggering a fireball.

Maybe the loud explosions were
The shrieks of vowels and consonants
Perennially silenced in the national anthem.

More poems have to be written.
Life has to go on.

Elegy for the slain bloggers

(Also P. Murugan)

You see some people are afraid of darkness
—Nyctophobia

You heard what happened to him?
So we have decided to collectively
Scream against this darkness,
Our sound waves collide.

If we are in sync
The troughs bottom up
The crests add up;
We are heard loud enough.

If our screams are
Not in sync
We cancel each other out
Our shadows intersect;
The void of the Umbra.

We become him.
Conform or perish

PART III
'LEARNING FROM THE PANTHERS'

Learning from the Panthers

(*A life in poems*)

> *Dalit panthers are the last chapter of Black panthers.*
> **—Anonymous**

Why do you write panther poetry?
I write panther poetry –people have the right to bear arms.

1
The Panthers aren't extinct.

We prowl the dense jungles.
We are disciplined men.
We upset the natural order of things.

2.
Slogans – rise up
Fly sky high like
The sky blue flag
The sky blue of universal brotherhood.

The panther prowls
With the swift gait of a bird in flight.

3.
We protect our own kind.
Always monopolize a local cliff
To get a wider view of the surroundings
Like birds flying ahead of the flock.

4.
The panthers march with an anthem
Like a gurgling evergreen epic
With tributaries branching out
Like blood coursing in the veins

of letters of the same vernacular
With different phonetics.

5.
Wild cats roar
as if to reclaim a lost world.
The bipedal panther
Stands erect with its gaze
Beyond the horizons.

6.
The picture hanging on the wall
Of the master of the martial arts
Who gave us the dictum
"*Educate Organize Agitate*".

7.
We will not let anyone else pronounce our names.
We will pronounce our names with the
Right intonation, enunciation.

We rework or crawl up
To the fortresses of lexicons
New coastlines for myths
Suddenly veering off course.

The panthers
Sharpen the claws
On barks of trees
Descending down to its rings
Documenting the duel.

Though we didn't like our names
We used to refer to ourselves in the third person.

Our name was the spine around which
Our world hinges.

8
Barren rocks
Amidst dense foliage of shrubs

Are receptacles of histories.
Approach them with respect
A panther
Might explode
From the shrubs.

The panthers march
Ahead of us
We foray into space
Between pages
In the time's crevasse
Not to trip on the
Shadow-lines of archaic monuments.

9.
Cops trail and tag
Our population
Fuel internal feuds
Force our extinction
To blow out the fire warming our souls.

10.
Swimming in an alien language
Is seeing ourselves
Or seeking our soul
In the deep sea's mirrors

Our tongue
Fenced with teeth like jagged rocks.

11.
The Panthers
always have their one paw
at the throat of an empire of
fluttering stars and stripes.

PART IV
LOVE AFTER BABEL

And the Lord said,
"Behold, the people is one and they have all one language ...
Go to, let us go down, and there confuse their language,
that they may not understand one
another's speech."
—**Genesis** XI: 6, 7.

(1)

A poem and its translation are
Like a pair of lopsided breasts,

One of them—a well-rounded cuss-word
The other—a pear-shaped sagging cliché.

(2)

I write from left to right.
She writes from right to left
(or vice versa).
Our calligraphy meets
The nadir of our abyss.

(3)

> *Novels, in general, were heterosexual,*
> *whereas poetry was completely homosexual;*
> *I guess short stories were bisexual,*
> *although he didn't say so.*
> —**Roberto Bolaño** *(Tr: Natasha Wimmer)*

When involved with a translated poem
In time's crevasse between word bricks
At abandoned construction sites,
I run the risk of outraging the modesty of some poetic forms.

(4)

During translations
Many rivers cross
The rolling spine of logic
Like birds perching on
Adjacent electric wires.

(5)

A translated poem is always *in-transit*
Like a flock of birds *in-flight*
Scripting a camaraderie in a cloudless sky.

Horizons dawn into blank pages.

(6)

Two love poems
From two different languages
Elope on a moonless night
Storming the Bastille
Of "apparently impregnable fortresses"
Of their syntax.

(7)

The uttered polysyllables of a monolithic empire
From a podium of an erect sprout of the rhetoric
the untranslatable geographies spread across time-zones
glued together with stitch marks-like railway-tracks.

(8)

REPETITION is TRANSLATION

Repetition like the dawn at every time zone,
Another utterance at another longitude-
A new hemisphere annexed to the empire
With every new translation.

(9)

> *Grammar is a form of history.*
> —**Derek Walcott**

The baton handed over
Like a cherry passed through
A prolonged lip-lock
A couplet transliterated into a new shade.

(10)

A translator is perennially in pursuit
Of his own rhythm, un-weaving his voice from the
Rhythmic wave-strokes on either shores.

(11)

Some poems are usurped
From their natal homes
They adorn the attire and learn the accent
Of their new homes
Shape-shifting themselves along the shadows of their better-halves
Like being inscribed into traditional meter and rhyme
With a vow of not uttering
A word in an alien tongue
Even at the pinnacle of ecstasy.

(12)

THE LANGUAGE OF THE SKIES

"Migrant bird script calligraphy
Of a nascent canon
In the comatose blue sky"—inspiration from a Malayalam poem.

Poetic forms like the sonnet or the Ghazal laundered and
Left to dry on the clothesline
Clouds imperfectly drift like a poem translated into free verse
Drenching us in tales from the other side of twilight.

Chisel oneself into a toiling wordsmith
Shape-shifting the body-text onto the diction
Tread the sky-clad coarse terrain.

The public-private tessellation
Woven into a second-skin garment
Like the tan lines on pale pigmentation.

(13)

In a bilingual edition, I see the poem
And its translation across the page
As if reclining on a double bed.

I always imagine a third poem
A perfect translation of the first
Like a statue of a woman
Chiselled in unwrinkled time.

(14)

The empire has ebbed
The not-so-emaciated waistline of a patriarch.
I see language in a dim twilight
Drawing its strength from its shadow
Like a tall yesteryear monument.

(15)

Wine brewed in freshly unearthed urns of time
From vineyards of "Grapes of Wrath"
Deferred dreams distilled and entombed in grey rain clouds
Drift into our open skies like newly translated poems.

(16)

AN EROTIC ENCOUNTER

After reading the poem aloud
smitten by her aftertaste

The translator approaches
the poem like a boy approaching
a girl on the dance floor.

They share a pelvic giggle,
a grinding dance
to the rhythm of their poems read aloud.

(17)

"Then all the nations of birds lifted together
the huge net of the shadows of this earth
in multitudinous dialects, twittering tongues,
stitching and crossing it."—Derek Walcott

Fiber-optically link the world like canals of
Online trade, Google-translate oneself
And trace yourself on Google earth,
It could take a long time for you to know who you are
Amidst the web traffic along world's sea routes.

(18)

The twilight of the empire
There is mismatch between the language-markets
Like winds of change from
An area of high to low pressure
Bullying flagpoles and pine trees.

The ship of conquest set sail
Along the sea-routes
Dropping anchor at every vernacular
(As if each vernacular were an undiscovered continent)

Naming all the foliage of the islands
Before annexing them to
An empire sans sunset.

After the empire has ebbed
The twilight is protracted too long
The sea-routes still remain
Like a stain of a dead oasis on a desert.

I am reminded of an evangelical church
In the shape of a ship's hull.

(19)

In an unnamed busy street
An occasional stranger
Elbows me like a cuss word grating
On my soul, I overhear a beggar
Seeking alms in my vernacular.

The language is an archipelago,
Its dialects are the islands
Slowly drifting apart like
Blood-relatives estranged to the vein
Until the sea swallows them
One at a time.

The market speaks the same language
Along the world's sea-routes.

(20)

MY LANGUAGE

The language we speak now,
Once had no fences;
Aggravated trespassing
Has rendered it barren.

At the frontiers of my language
Deployed with an insidious intent
Is a domesticated erstwhile stray-dog
With its bark worse than its bite;
But carefully tethered to harm no one.

If you frequent my tongue
The rust on your tongue-cleaner
Can cause tetanus to your soul.

Introducing an alien tongue in elementary schools
Is like building dams on rivers
Too close to their origins.
The river will be sedated for eternity.

In the autobiography of my vernacular
There were a few suicide notes
Transliterated with an indelible ink
Like the legacy of slave owners
Passed on to the hardbound of my poetry book
-once a stepping pedestal for imperial boots.

My language
Was a tax-free transit point
At one of the world's shores
Like the Cape of Good Hope.

Now, history of mankind
Snores in my language.

A POSTHUMOUS LETTER

The specific traits of a Society correspond exactly to the untranslatable locutions of its language.
Black Orpheus—**John Paul Sartre** (tr John Macombie)

I am a primate
dwelling in the wild forests
of my language.

My tongue lost irretrievably
in the swamp of hunger,
I hide amidst the barren rocks.

Your own selfie
sheds light on the swastikas
dangling like a locket
when you hide in the interstices of your alphabet.

My name had been a museum piece
Heaving my last breath like my dialect
before and after you live-streamed my scream.
("the tyranny of real time")

My language is an extinct variety of paddy.
It doesn't sprout in the clay used to sculpt my body.

I am a martyr of my language!

(22)

ACCIDENT AT A RIVER
Accident Following Wrangling Over Naming of Rivulets

Staff Reporter

KABANI, Nov 5 Twenty bodies of poets and translators were recovered from the shores of a river near the state capital. The bodies were like couplets intertwined and the river crisscrossed the border between two states built along "thoughts on linguistic states".. The camp director had warned the participants of the translation workshop that spirits of other participants could leap into theirs and each of them were given aliases like a plastic steering oar that never yields to either (up or down) streams of the river. The poets claimed that to be baptized in a form of poetry in another language, it was necessary to nose-dive into a particular river. Some of the translators were also language teachers – they allegedly danced on the hanging bride hoping that their students weren't around. Another prospective reason for the onset of the wrangle was that poets demanded dope – during their short recesses. They insisted that poems be written and consumed in the same tongue, like dope bought directly from the source before being chopped up. Some poets may have died due to narcotic overdose – can only be confirmed after autopsy reports are made public.

Afterword

ANANYA WILSON-BHATTACHARYA

> *They ask me why do you write poems?*
> *I write poems—the people have the right to ...bear arms.*

These lines, taken from his one-stanza masterpiece 'Why Do I Write Poetry?', encapsulate the very essence of Chandramohan S' approach to his craft in his third collection, *Love after Babel and Other Poems*. These poems are unapologetically weapons, fighting against the pre-modern notion of caste in all its insidious 21st century glory.

Reading the collection, one is struck by the undeniably political tone and content of the poems. Chandramohan's position as a Dalit writer illuminates his treatment of caste-based oppression, whilst also creating a sense of radical solidarity between various marginalized identities in contemporary Indian society through his focus on other forms of oppression, namely on experiences of Islamophobia. His poetry speaks for itself, and will never become irrelevant because it acknowledges the ever-changing nature of the society it is concerned with. It deals with age-old structures and their modern, subtle manifestations in everyday life. As Deeptha Achar has pointed out in her introduction to his previous collection, *Letters to Namdeo Dhasal*—which contained many of the same poems, including some earlier versions – Chandramohan 'renders caste as a contemporary category'.

It is impossible to overlook the precision of this collection—precision of setting, of time, of perspective. There is no sense of the often-used maxim of poetry that ambiguity is everything, and all poems must be open to interpretation. The language is extremely powerful, and often metaphorical, but it makes no claims to ambiguity. It looks the reader straight in the eye and tells them its experiences. It adopts certain perspectives—Dalit, Muslim, particular gender identities within these—with a specific purpose of resistance which requires a direct and often factual tone.

'A Local Train Conversation', for example, is a poem encompassing a particular subject about which we know we will be learning from the title itself. This poem—which has two versions with some slightly different imagery—is hugely context-specific; it is an open rejection of any false claims to universality which are often demanded by mainstream poetry critique. Chandramohan has placed us in the specific setting of an Indian local train, with its inevitably diverse passengers, from the outset, and it is within this frame that we must remain in our reading.

Throughout the poem the reader is confronted with the sheer physical discomfort of the speaker, expressed through the metaphor of cricket. The 'Pakistani fast bowler' seated opposite him is the perpetrator of this particular instance of a much wider oppression. This is encompassed within the image of physical violence: 'Though seated opposite me/ I can feel him charging on to me'—as a metaphor for the bowler's scrutinizing of the speaker in trying to figure out his identity. But despite his apprehension, the speaker holds a sardonic understanding of his opponent in this game of cricket: he is 'Camouflaged in a three-piece suit/And anglicized accent'. Something has been taken from the man opposite, something has been done to him, the verbs tell us; he has been camouflaged and Anglicized. The speaker is prevented from embracing his (implicitly) lower-caste heritage, but so is the 'bowler'; he is a victim of colonialism. The speaker wishes to be camouflaged, while simultaneously recognizing that this is not to achieve true emancipation, to be able to express one's authentic self, but simply the best option for survival in a society layered with complex systems of oppression. This is just one example of how Chandramohan's poems are never only concerned with one identity, with one perspective, but with the multiple and multi-layered experiences lived in South Asia every day.

Indeed, this focus on a broad range of experiences, combined with the clearly radical politics of many of the poems in the collection, not only singles Chandramohan out among young up-and-coming poets in India, but also locates him within a wide movement of resistance against India's current Hindu right government—one in which new alliances among the oppressed are being forged in order to protest an increasingly fascistic regime. It is his embrace of these alliances, as well as his positioning at the intersection of Left and Dalit politics, across his poems that renders Chandramohan such a subversive figure at this particular moment, and makes his rise to prominence within contemporary Indian poetry in English all the more intriguing.

'Beef poem' illustrates this point perfectly, situating Chandramohan's writing even more specifically within the current Indian political climate, where the condemnation of beef-eating in the name of 'cow protection' has become one of the major lines along which government-affiliated thugs carry out attacks on Muslims and Dalits. Chandramohan's own position in relation to this phenomenon is crystallized in the second stanza: 'Mastheads with nausea/ Against beef eating/ Consider my poems/ "*untouchable*"'. This 'untouchability' of his poems points to the discomfort they would inevitably cause to these mainstream media 'mastheads', but more explicitly, to the historically 'untouchable' status of Dalits in India, and in turn to the intensification of caste-based oppression which is an important and ugly aspect of the rise to power of the Hindu right in recent years. The lines 'When I manoeuvre sharp curves of history/ In my rear-view mirror', a variation of which can be found in 'Thirteen Ways of Looking at a Black Beard', indicate the importance of this political 'history' in the poet's consideration of everyday objects—be it beef or beards.

'The Rape and Murder of a Tribal' engages with another, equally important facet of the enduring presence of India's oppressive history: national silence in response to gendered violence against women from the most marginalized groups in Indian society. The poem adopts a highly intersectional approach in examining, through a pulsing repeated negative, the complete denial of justice for these women—from official mourning processes to legal procedures – and their erasure from mainstream feminist activism. 'No youth were roused to protests…No Prime minister addressed the nation…No police officials were transferred and suspended…No billion women rising'. Perhaps most tellingly—a line which ties in with Chandramohan's interrogation, across the collection, of India's collective consciousness—'No nation's conscience was haunted'.

Chandramohan does extend the realm of perspective beyond South

Asia to the rest of the world. The collection's opening chapter, entitled 'Call me Ishmail', contains an epigraph by Hayan Charara entitled 'Being Arab', clearly underlining the vantage point of the poems to follow. 'Thirteen Ways of Looking at a Black Beard'—the second poem in this chapter—positions us in a harsh present-day setting with a nostalgic outlook on an era 'Before the twin towers fell', before Islamophobia reached its current heights in which a man's beard can render him a target at immigration control. Chandramohan opens his poem with 'the razor, shaving/hundreds of beards', a symbol of forced self-repression on the part of Muslims the world over in the face of such stigma. The metaphor of language, which becomes prominent later in the collection, appears here: 'Shave your dreadlocks. /Your bald head/ Is an evacuated language', evoking the gradual erasure of language and culture through colonialism. This is further emphasized by the following lines: 'Now try locating your home/On Google Earth', a theme invoked one stanza later by 'The blade is...to redraw maps'. This poem is not one person's experience; rather, it sets Islamophobia firmly within a contemporary global framework. Chandramohan does not stop here. He extends the subject matter and timespan of the poem to when 'Some islands changed hands/Between their imperial masters', making even more explicit the geopolitical dynamics underlying such everyday airport experiences. Here is an urgent reminder to the reader, through the invocation of historical events, not to forget the most crucial aspect of modern-day Islamophobia: the culpability of Western powers both in promoting terrorism and in the persecution of Muslims on the grounds of this terrorism. The poem has no qualms about declaring its anti-imperialist politics openly and boldly.

This poem's female-centric counterpart, 'Thirteen Ways of Looking at a Black Burkini', which in fact opens the collection, was shortlisted for the Srinivas Rayaprol Poetry Prize in 2016. This poem brings the question of Islamophobia even more up to date with its focus on a garment designed, in recent years, by and for Muslim women, once again demonstrating the broad scope of marginalized perspectives Chandramohan considers, which renders him distinct among Dalit poets in India today.

This collection also demonstrates Chandramohan's highly political approach to language and the act of writing poetry itself (as signified by the simple, self-explanatory title of the collection's second chapter, 'The Word'). Many poems in this section use the metaphor of poetry to make political statements, for example 'The Immigrant Word'. This poem constitutes one of Chandramohan's most explicit discussions of the ostracization and humiliation often endured by immigrants, describing the 'immigrant experience for/A word in a poem' through a series of disturbingly real human immigrant experiences. Some of these are poignantly and beautifully woven into the extended metaphor, for example 'solitary confinement/ In the prison of syntax', and 'being subjected to numerous enunciations/At poetry slams' which ingeniously invokes the all-too common mispronunciation of non-Western names which immigrants and people of colour continue to endure.

This political approach to language is both explored and perfectly illustrated by the final poem of the collection, the titular, 22-section 'Love After Babel', which examines the art of translation through a wide variety of poignant metaphors, resulting in a tone at once romantic, historical and political. Chandramohan's concern with the relationship between language and colonialism becomes clear in stanza 14 of this poem, which begins 'the empire has ebbed'. The stanza invokes some form of awakening from the colonial suppression of language, of a new beginning in which the poet sees language 'in a dim twilight/ Drawing its strength from its shadow'. These lines illustrate the gradual development of new linguistic identity in a post-colonial world, still 'dim' at this moment, while simultaneously raising a crucial point—that translation is inevitably shaped by the 'shadow' of the original language.

Indeed, this 'twilight' seems to represent the process of translation itself, as suggested by the couplet near the end of the poem: 'Clouds imperfectly drift like a poem translated into free verse/Drenching us in tales from the other side of twilight'. Here, Chandramohan vividly evokes the way in which these 'tales' are conveyed across languages, through translation. In stark contrast to some of the descriptions of translation earlier in the poem as careful, precise and even hesitant, these lines create a sense of translation as somewhat uncontrolled, 'imperfect', fueling the flow of literature—of ideas—between cultures, unleashing the irregularity of 'free verse' in this process of unapologetic 'drenching'.

The global nature of the translation which concerns the poet is encompassed by the mention of 'poetic forms like the sonnet or the Ghazal' in this section, a reminder of the overlapping features of these two forms, without undermining the sense of inequality between them in terms of their global authority or readership. In line with his poetic mission to counter this imbalance, Chandramohan overtly illustrates his theme by citing 'inspiration from a Malayalam poem' after the following beautiful stanza:

> Migrant bird script calligraphy
> Of a nascent canon
> In the comatose blue sky.

Tellingly, this is not a direct translation, only taking 'inspiration'. The reader cannot fully know how far all the ideas evoked in these three lines— around migration, death, and freedom, all touched on in relation to the broader theme of language—are present in the same way in the original Malayalam poem cited, but perhaps Chandramohan is telling us that that is not the point. The ideas may well have developed in the English translation, have been expressed differently, while never losing their fundamental inspiration, and this new expression of ideas is the effect created by the 'twilight' of translation with which Chandramohan's poem is concerned.

The final section of the poem 'Love After Babel' – and of the entire collection—is fittingly entitled 'A Posthumous Letter', and describes the poet's relationship with his native language, to which he proclaims his enduring loyalty in a post-colonial world, despite the forces of colonialism and globalisation attempting to erase such connections. The poet leaves his readers with the haunting declaration: 'I am a martyr of my language!' This final line of the collection provides a conception of the role of poets from marginalised backgrounds: to defend their cultures, as represented by their languages, at the potential cost of mainstream popularity, universal palatability or recognition as canonical.

While many writers—including poets—may use their work to celebrate hybrid identities and the sharing of language and culture, particularly across the global North-South divide, Chandramohan's treatment of these themes—as both discussed and demonstrated in his poems—does not carry any pretensions of this liberalism, instead being crafted as an active political tool to counter multiple forms of oppression in India and across the world.

Ananya Wilson-Bhattacharya[1]

---

1. Ananya Wilson-Bhattacharya is a writer and activist. Her interests include Indian and UK politics, questions of racism, intersectional and Marxist feminism and literature by marginalized writers. She tweets @AnanyaWilson.

About the author

Chandramohan S (Sathyanathan) is a Dalit Indian poet, short story writer and a social critique based in the south Indian state of Kerala. He is pursuing research in mathematics, apart from being a translator, editor and a social activist. He is a member of the P.K. Rosi foundation, a cultural collective (named after the legendary, pioneering Dalit actress) that seeks to demarginalize Dalit-Bahujans. His poetry collections *Warscape Verses* (2014) and *Letters to Namdeo Dhasal* (2016), were shortlisted for the *Srinivas Rayaprol Poetry Prize* and the *Harish Govind Memorial Prize.*

Chandramohan coordinates English-language poetry readings in Kerala as well as a subaltern cultural collective there; in 2016 *Outlook Magazine* listed him as Dalit Achiever of the Year.

www.ingramcontent.com/pod-product-compliance
Lightning Source LLC
Chambersburg PA
CBHW071249070526
44583CB00017B/2399